Cambridge Early Years

Communication and Language
for English as a Second Language

Learner's Book 2A

Claire Medwell

Contents

Note to parents and practitioners   3

Block 1: Friends, family and me   4

Block 2: Home and buildings   18

Acknowledgements   32

Note to parents and practitioners

This Learner's Book provides activities to support the first term of ESL Communication and Language for Cambridge Early Years 2.

Activities can be used at school or at home. Children will need support from an adult. Additional guidance about activities can be found in the **For practitioners** boxes.

Stories are provided for children to enjoy looking at and listening to. Children are not expected to be able to read the stories themselves.

Children will encounter the following characters within this book. You could ask children to point to the characters when they see them on the pages, and say their names.

The Learner's Book activities support the Teaching Resource activities. The Teaching Resource provides step-by-step coverage of the Cambridge Early Years curriculum and guidance on how the Learner's Book activities develop the curriculum learning statements.

Hi, my name is Mia.

Find us on the front covers doing lots of fun activities.

Hi, my name is Gemi.

Hi, my name is Rafi.

Hi, my name is Kiho.

Block 1 Friends, family and me

Family Finger Rhyme Traditional children's rhyme

Daddy finger, Daddy finger
Where are you?
Here I am, here I am! How are you?

Mummy finger, Mummy finger
Where are you?
Here I am, here I am! How are you?

Sister finger, Sister finger
Where are you?
Here I am, here I am! How are you?

Brother finger, brother finger
Where are you?
Here I am, here I am! How are you?

Baby finger, Baby finger
Where are you?
Here I am, here I am! How are you?

I spy!

Count and say.

Count and circle the different family members in the picture.

1   2   3   4   5

For practitioners

Ask *How many mums can you see?* Children circle the mums and the matching number. Encourage children to say the number and name of the family member, e.g., *four mums*. Repeat for the other family members using different colours.

Our Families

There are big families,

There are families with lots of brothers …
And there are families with lots of sisters.

Then there are families with brothers *and* sisters!
Others just have mum and dad.

There are children who live with their grandma and grandpa.
There are children who live with their dad.

And others who live with their mum.

There are families who have babies to play with ...
And others who have pets.
Some have lots of pets, or just one pet, like a cat or a tiny fish!

Point to the 'funny' pets.

There are children who live in cities,
And others who live in the country.
There are children who live near their cousins,
And others who live far apart.

It doesn't matter how big or how small your family is,
Where you live,
Or who you live with …

Families are very special … and so are YOU!

My family

Draw and say.

Look at the example. Draw the faces of your family in the other windows of the house.

This is my brother!

For practitioners

Invite children to point to the window in the house where they can see the chameleon waving. Ask *Whose brother is it?* (Kiho's.) Children then draw members of their own family in the remaining windows and talk about them in pairs.

Which picture?

Listen and mark.

Choose the picture that matches what you hear.

There are big families.

There are families with lots of sisters.

There are families who have babies to play with.

There are families who live in cities.

> **For practitioners**
> Ask children what they can see in the pictures. Read the sentences aloud. Children mark the picture that matches the sentence.

Story map: Our Families

Listen to the story.

Point to the pictures and retell the story. Then join the dots.

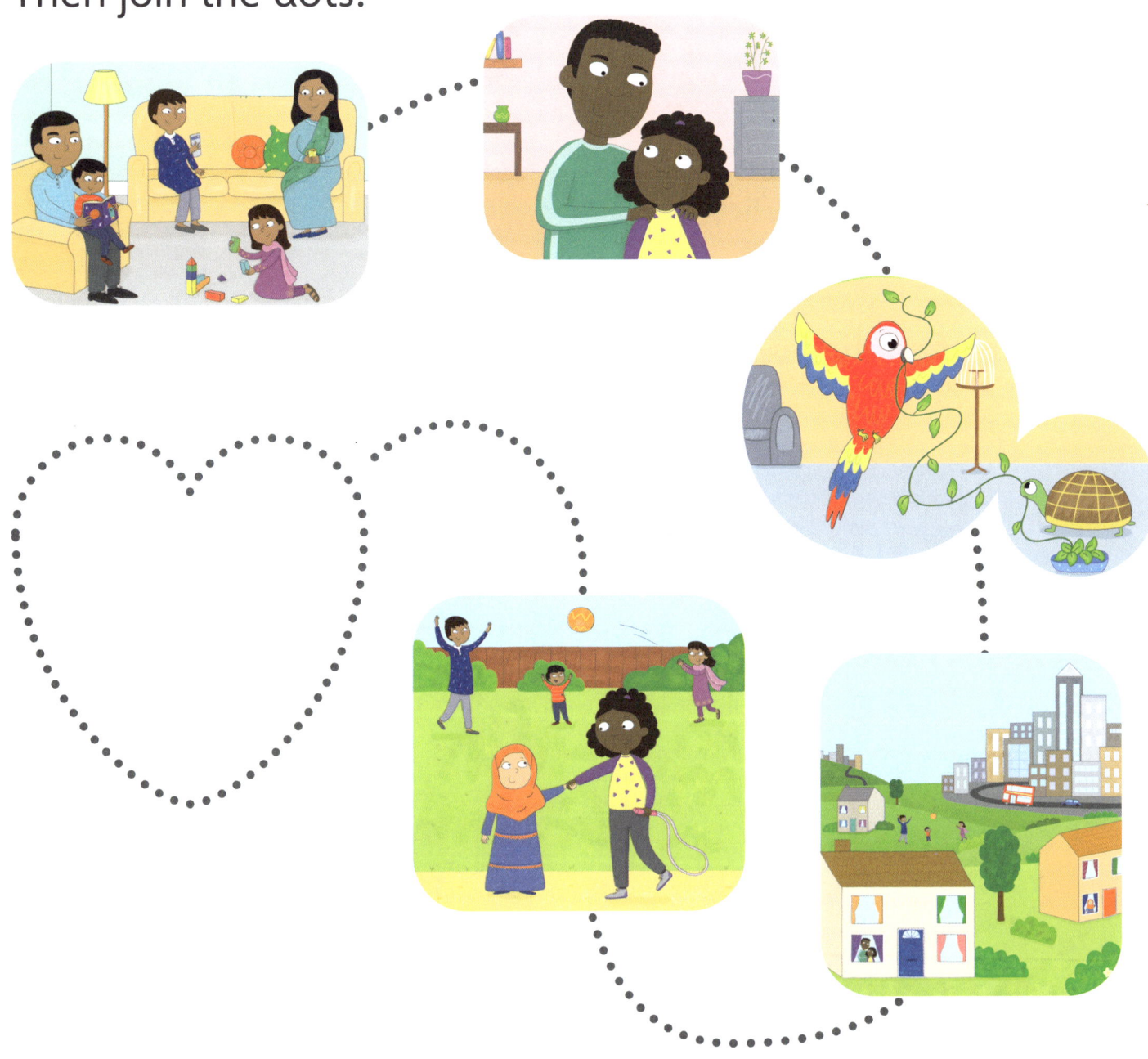

For practitioners
Read the story aloud. In pairs, children retell the story using simple words and phrases with the help of the story map. Ask children to join the dots at the end and identify the shape.

Our clothes

Point and say.

Name the family members.
Match the clothes to the family members.

a pink coat — brown trousers — a green jumper — a yellow dress — a red hat — a blue shirt

For practitioners

Children point to the family members in the picture and say who they are. They then match the clothes in the box to the family member wearing them. Encourage them to say the name and colour, e.g. *a green jumper*.

Happy families

Spot the difference.

Name the family members. Find and circle the differences.

For practitioners

Children identify the family members. Talk about what they are wearing. Invite the children to spot and circle the differences in each picture and talk about what they are wearing.

Let's run!

Listen and mark.

Match the action to the correct family member.

For practitioners

Say each phrase out loud and give children time to trace or mark a line from the action to the correct family member: *Skip to baby. Hop to mummy. Run to sister. Walk to daddy. Jump to brother.*

Block 2 Home and buildings

My Friendly Spider

I have a friendly spider,
She lives inside my bath.
She runs around in circles,
And makes me laugh and laugh!
She gets very dizzy,
And looks at me so strange,
And before I can count to three …
1 … 2 … She runs back down the drain!

I have a friendly spider,
She lives above my bed.
She catches flies,
And gives high fives,
And spins her little web!

I have a friendly spider,
She lives in my play box.
She gives me toys,
Which make a loud noise …
BEEP BEEP! BRUM BRUM! CHOO CHOO!
Then hides behind the blocks!

Where is the spider?

Draw and say.

Draw a spider *in*, *on* or *under* the objects.

I'm on the table!

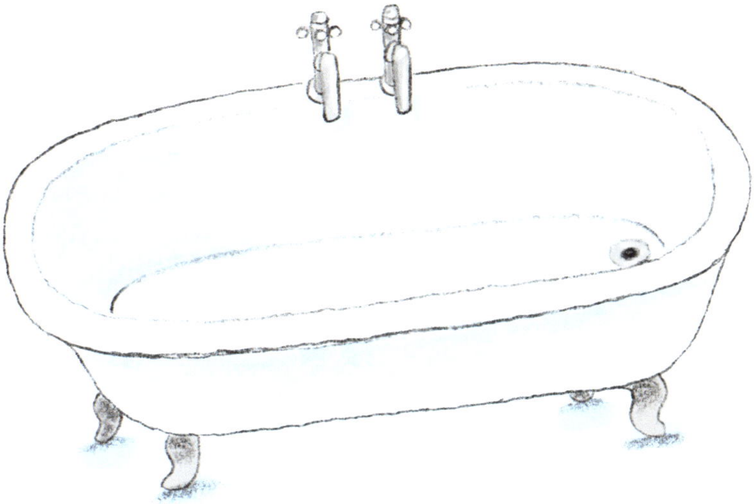

For practitioners

Children draw their spiders *in*, *on* or *under* the objects and describe the location.

In the City by Dominika Lipniewska

The city wakes up slowly.

Soon everything moves very fast

in the hustle and bustle of the morning rush.

In the city, you can find buildings that are tall

and some that are small.

There are places to go that are green and leafy where you can find creatures of all sizes.

How many can you spot?

The people are all very different

but they often like the same things.

The city can be a very noisy place.

What a lot of sounds!

Which one do you think is the loudest?

In the city, people travel around in different ways.

Which vehicles have you been in?

At the zoo, you can see amazing animals that don't come from the city but can teach us about nature.

People in the city have many different jobs.

Which ones do you know?

At night, some parts of the city are fast asleep

Shhh!

But not everyone sleeps at night.
Who is still awake?

At sunrise, everything wakes up again to start another busy day in the city.

In the City

Match and say.

Find the matching building in the city picture. Say the colour.

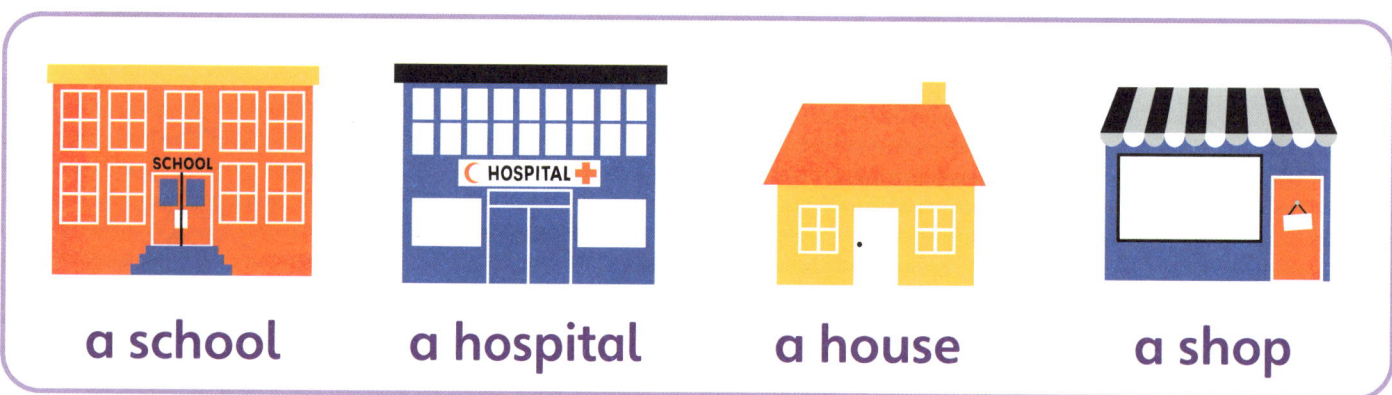

a school   a hospital   a house   a shop

For practitioners

Children find the matching buildings in the city picture and say the colours. Encourage them to talk about buildings and colours they know. Naming each building using words will support their understanding.

A shape building

Match and colour.

Find and colour the matching shapes.

For practitioners
Children match the shapes to the coloured examples and then colour them in the correct colours. Prompt talk about the colours and shapes by asking questions, e.g., *What colour is this shape? How many yellow shapes are there?*

Let's build!

Look and make.

Choose some blocks and make a building.

For practitioners

Children choose a simple building to make using construction blocks. Encourage children to describe their building as they make it.

My transport

Listen and circle.

Listen to the questions and circle ✔ or ✘ for each one. Draw your favourite transport.

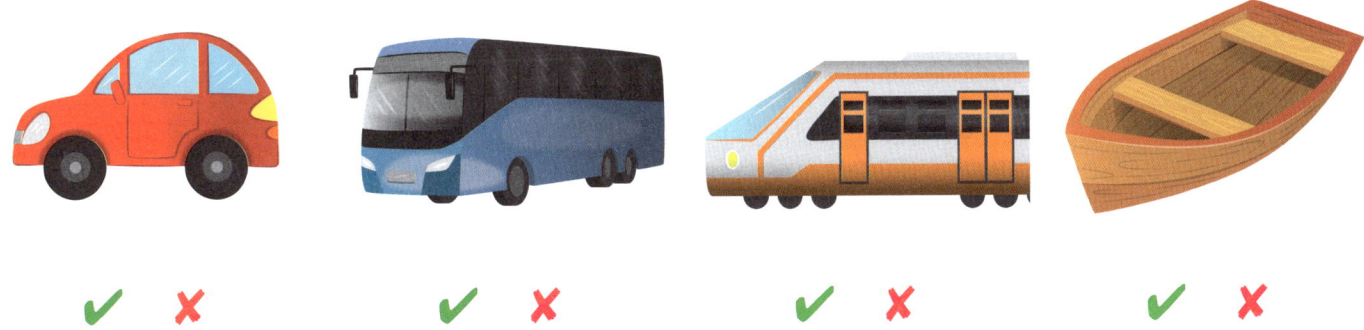

✔ ✘   ✔ ✘   ✔ ✘   ✔ ✘

For practitioners

Ask *Do you travel by car / bus / train / boat*? Allow time after each question for children to circle the tick or cross under the picture. Children can draw their favourite transport in the space provided and talk about it.

Mia's favourite transport

Join the dots.

Join the dots to see Mia's favourite transport.

For practitioners
Children look at the picture and predict how Mia likes to travel. Children then join the dots to discover her favourite transport.

Traffic lights

Trace and colour.

Complete and colour the traffic light.

Stop!   Slow down!   Go!

For practitioners
Children trace and colour the traffic light using the photo of the traffic light as their guide. Encourage children to point to the colours in the traffic signs. Say the corresponding action words *Stop*, *Slow down* and *Go!* when pointing at each traffic light colour to reinforce understanding.

Acknowledgements

The authors and publishers acknowledge the following sources of copyright material and are grateful for the permissions granted.
While every effort has been made, it has not always been possible to identify the sources of all the material used, or to trace all copyright holders.
If any omissions are brought to our notice, we will be happy to include the appropriate acknowledgements on reprinting.

In the City Illustrations © Dominka Lipniewska, 2019; copyright in the work © GMC Publications Ltd., 2019

Thanks to the following for permission to reproduce images:

p28 popovaphoto/Getty Images, p31 seraficus/Getty Images

Thanks to the following artists at Beehive Illustration:

Laura Arias, Tamara Joubert, Alice Larsson, Michelle McGovern, Sarah Pitt, Claire Philpott, Jan Smith.

Cover characters by Becky Davies (The Bright Agency)